Whale Rescue!

written by Karen Edwards

McGraw-Hill
School Division

New York   Farmington

Winter came early in the Arctic that year. Ice formed on the calm sea, trapping three gray whales near Point Barrow, Alaska. As the rest of the pod swam south, these three could not reach the open sea. They would probably die beneath the ice. Every year, some whales die this way in the Arctic, but not this time. Instead, a team of 100 people worked for almost three weeks to free the whales. All over the world, people watched the rescue on television. They wondered, "Will the whales be saved?"

Whales are mammals like people. Unlike fish, they cannot breathe underwater. They come to the surface to breathe.

Inuit, or Eskimo, fishermen discovered the three gray whales on October 7, 1988. One adult whale and two younger whales were in two small pools of water, that were completely surrounded by ice. The only way the whales could get any air was by pushing up through the small pools of water.

Beaufort Sea

Point Barrow

Alaska

Before winter comes, gray whales swim south. They travel through the Beaufort Sea to the vast Pacific Ocean near Mexico. These whales had waited too long to leave the area. A sudden drop in the temperature had frozen the waters around where the whales were feeding and trapped them.

News of the whales' problem spread quickly. An oil company 200 miles away in Prudhoe Bay sent a heavy, flat boat called a barge. Everyone hoped that it could smash through the ice and make a path for the whales to swim out.

The Inuit knew they could not wait for the barge to arrive because the whales needed more room to breathe—now. They went to work, using chain saws to chop blocks of ice and make the air holes bigger. Then they pushed the blocks under the sea ice with poles. They didn't want the whales to hit the ice blocks when they came up for air.

More helpers flew to Point Barrow. Ron Morris, a biologist from the U.S. Fisheries Service, took charge of the rescue. The rescue team was unusual, people who held different ideas about the value of whales joined together. The team included people from save-the-whale groups and biologists. Whale hunters and oil companies, which have sometimes hurt whales in oil spills, also lent their support.

One thing the whales got plenty of was
love. When they poked their noses above the
water, people patted them and talked to them.
They even gave the whales names. The Inuit
named them Putu (Ice Hole), Siku (Ice), and
Kanik (Snowflake), and the biologists named
them Bonnet, Crossbeak, and Bone.

The team kept chopping the ice to keep the breathing holes open. It was difficult work because of the freezing weather and the snow. The team hardly had time to swallow their own quick meals.

The rescue team had been working for twelve days when two young men from Minnesota decided to try a new plan. They spent their own money to fly to Point Barrow with special machines, called de-icers. These are somewhat like large electric fans that can be used in water. The de-icers stirred up the deep water by bringing up warmer water from below, which helped ice from forming.

The plan worked as the warmer water helped keep the air holes open.

The team noticed that the whales liked the warmer water, and they didn't seem to mind the noise of the machines. This success led to a new plan, which was to make a path of holes through the ice leading toward the sea. They would use the de-icers to warm them up, hoping the whales would follow the path from hole to hole. This way they would be able to get air as they went.

There was bad news to come, however. The whale called Bone had disappeared under the ice. The team sadly concluded that Bone had died. Then they learned that the oil barge was stuck in the ice and wouldn't be able to reach them.

The team had to try something else. Special helicopters were brought in, which dropped concrete blocks weighing 9,000 pounds to try to break apart the ice. Again, people worried that the sound would upset the whales or that the concrete blocks would hurt them.

Still another danger faced the whales: polar bears. Polar bears feast on fish and seals. What would happen if a polar bear discovered the trapped whales? Ron Morris said that he would not save the whales from polar bears. After all, bears are another group of animals that need to be protected. It would not be right, he thought, to kill one animal in order to save another.

Point Barrow, Alaska is not far from Siberia. In 1988, Siberia was part of the Soviet Union and is now in Russia. Soviet ships were working in the Arctic Ocean. The Soviets told the United States that they would send two ships to help— strong, heavy ships called icebreakers. This was great news for the rescue team.

The first ship took almost a whole day to smash through the ice. Not all of the ice was flat. Near the open water there was a hill of ice 30 feet high and 1,200 feet wide. The second ship, the *Vladimir Arseniev*, finished the job. It broke a path through the ice that almost reached the whales.

The *Vladimir Arseniev* was greeted by 200 cheering people when it reached Point Barrow. People were happy to see that it was flying both the American and the Soviet flags. The two countries were working together to save the whales.

Everyone on the team breathed a sigh of relief. Arnold Brower, Jr., an Alaskan boat captain, said, "I feel like my burden is lifted."

At last the whales could escape to the sea, but surprisingly, they didn't. It seemed to the rescuers like the whales didn't want to leave. Ron Morris, thinking that the crowds of people might be bothering the whales, closed the area.

Hours passed, and still the whales didn't take the hint. "I thought they'd be gone by now," said Ron Morris. What could the team do?

People from the group Greenpeace thought they could lead the whales out by playing recordings of whale sounds. Another idea was to play the sounds that orcas make. The team hoped the "killer whales" would scare the gray whales into the ocean.

Finally, it just took a little time. Putu and Siku stayed in the channel for more than a day, but on October 27, the larger whale swam into the open water. About an hour later, it swam back to get the smaller whale.

The exhausted but happy rescue team wished the whales good luck. The two gray whales had thousands of miles to swim before their journey was over, but they had been saved.

Story Questions and Activity

1. When and where does this story take place?

2. Would the Inuit have been able to save the whales alone?

3. Why did so many people want to help save whales?

4. What is the main idea of the book?

5. How do you think the gray whales in this story would describe their rescue to the blue whale in *Big Blue Whale*?

Figure It Out!

On page 13, you read that a crowd of 200 people cheered the ship when it reached Point Barrow. 100 people were part of the rescue team. If 30 people were news reporters, and the rest were helpers, how many people were helpers? Write two or three sentences that tell how you found the answer.

McGRAW-HILL READING

McGraw-Hill School Division 🪐

A Division of The **McGraw·Hill** *Companies*

ISBN 0-02-185180-8

9 780021 851805